MW01174128

The Law of Gravity

The Law of Gravity

Olivier Sylvestre

Translated by Bobby Theodore

Playwrights Canada Press

TORONTO

LIBRARY AND ARCHIVES CANADA CATALOGUING IN PUBLICATION
Title: The law of gravity / Olivier Sylvestre ; translated by Bobby Theodore.
Other titles: La loi de la gravité. English
Names: Sylvestre, Olivier, author. | Theodore, Bobby, translator.
Description: A play. | Translation of: La loi de la gravité.
Identifiers: Canadiana (print) 20210161388 | Canadiana (ebook) 20210161469 | ISBN 9780369101693 (softcover) | ISBN 9780369101709 (PDF) | ISBN 9780369101716 (HTML) | ISBN 9780369101723 (Kindle)
Classification: LCC PS8637.Y447 L83413 2021 | DDC C842/.6—dc23

Playwrights Canada Press operates on Mississaugas of the Credit, Wendat, Anishinaabe, Métis, and Haudenosaunee land. It always was and always will be Indigenous land.

We acknowledge the financial support of the Canada Council for the Arts, the Ontario Arts Council (OAC), Ontario Creates, and the Government of Canada for our publishing activities.

Canada Council for the Arts   Conseil des arts du Canada

ONTARIO ARTS COUNCIL
CONSEIL DES ARTS DE L'ONTARIO
an Ontario government agency
un organisme du gouvernement de l'Ontario

ONTARIO CREATES | ONTARIO CRÉATIF

For my friend Max D, the spark that brought
Dom and Fred to life.

La loi de la gravité was first produced by Youtheatre at the Segal Centre for Performing Arts, Montreal, on January 9, 2017, followed by a school tour. It featured the following cast and creative team:

Actors: Aisha Jarvis and Laurent McCuaig-Pitre

Director: Frédéric Sasseville-Painchaud
Lighting Design: Martin Sirois
Sound Design: Maxime Corbeil-Perron
Costume Design: Cynthia St-Gelais
Stage Manager: Frédérique Folly

The play was later produced in French by Compagnie La Nuit te soupire and le Festival des francophonies en Limousin on February 28, 2017, at Théâtre La Loge, Paris, with the following cast and creative team:

Actors: Alison Valence and Quentin Laugier

Director: Anthony Thibault
Artistic Collaboration: Louise Dudek
Sound Design: Elisa Monteil
Video Design: Boris Carré

Characters

Dom: Baseball cap, buzz cut, overalls, and a sweatshirt. The hardened look of someone who's already been through a lot.

Fred: Long hair, black clothes, leather jacket, gloomy look. Someone who seems like they're trying to disappear.

This is the story of DOM *and* FRED.
And the famous Letters, the big white Letters, on the hillside next to the bridge, towering like a monument.
Garbage, empty beer cases . . . it's a perfect spot.
The Letters spell out the words: Not-The-City.
It's pretty ugly.
But there's something welcoming . . . it's a hiding place, a refuge of sorts.

This also the story of the cliff, right beside The Letters, that plunges into the river.
And of the rows of houses, thousands of them, just behind.
And of The City, right over there, on the other side of the river.
And of the birds, watching constantly from up above.
And of the bridge, a guard dog, deciding who gets to cross or not.

DOM *and* FRED, *yeah, this is them.*
They're fourteen years old.
They're beautiful.

Prologue

DOM takes a step forward, alone, facing the emptiness, ball cap pulled down, at the entrance to the bridge.

DOM
Here I am, all alone, about to cross the bridge.
Worst night of my life since learning the alphabet.
Everything hurts, everywhere, under my skin.
I gotta get the fuck out of here.
I'm all set. Ready as I'll ever get.
I'm shaking, freezing cold, and soaking wet.
The City's calling from the other side—*come here, come here.*
And the bridge is up there, watching me.
What are you looking at, Bridge?
I'll cross you if I want to, okay!
So why haven't I?
Just watch me!
I take a step forward.
The City lights twinkle faintly, far away.

There's a low rumbling noise, like a big dog growling.

All of a sudden everything starts to shake.
And there's this growling, like, like—a big dog!

You don't scare me, Bridge!
I move forward.
I move forward.
I don't go back.
But with every step, The City is a bit further away.
And then . . .

> *The growling gets louder and spotlights blind* DOM.
> DOM *screams.*
> *We no longer see anything.*

1. The Wrong Side

DOM
Okay so
this is how it starts.

FRED
This story

DOM
On the third of September.

FRED
Grade 9, fourteen, not fifteen, not yet.

DOM
Here I am—
on the edge of the cliff

with the big white Letters
you can see from far away
like big white teeth,
a beacon, informing the world what's here, over on this side—
NOT–THE–CITY.

FRED
I'm new here—
It's all lawns, pools, prefab houses, golden retrievers, muscle cars
far as the eye can see.
There's even a replica rocket that'll never take off,
right in the middle of the highway.
Help. Me. Please.

DOM
Birds are circling around me.
Hey, guys . . . Knock it off. I'm not a french fry, okay.
I look across the river, at what's on the other side—factories,
promises.
The City.
I'd fly over there if I were like you.
I'm *hopeless*.

FRED
After we're moved in, I log on,
looking for a friend.

DOM
School's called Happy Hills.
The name's enough to make you hurl.
And just as I'm thinking that—

FRED
Hey. How's it going?

Pause.

DOM
Who are you, what do you want, I don't even know you.

FRED
We just got here.
Me, my father, and my brother Bruno.
You in 4-E?

DOM
Oh, God. You too?

FRED
You're the first person I've talked to—I don't know anything about this place.

Pause.

DOM
Really?

FRED
You wanna be friends?

DOM
I'm warning you—I never laugh, I have no friends,
and I hate everything everyone else likes.
Any questions?

FRED
Several.
First—where can you get
decent shoes around here?

DOM
Don't tell me someone with actual taste
just moved to Not-The-City?

FRED
Second—where's the highest spot
to look at the stars?

DOM
Do you have a third?

FRED
Not yet. But it's coming.

DOM
I tell him I know a place—the big Letters.
At the top of the cliff, close to the bridge,
advertising our disaster of a non-city to the world.
But I'm warning you, the path there is steep, dirty,
and desperate, full of twists and turns, and totally muddy.
You're gonna scream and swear at the whole world.

FRED
Sounds awesome!

DOM
Yeah, well . . .

Pause.

Okay. Sending you the location.

FRED
Dom and Fred are now friends.

DOM
See that pile of empties?
Go until the busted tires,
watch out for the dog shit,
go past the dead oak,
cross the ravine,
follow the trail of used rubbers,
climb the rocks.
Be careful, don't fall.

FRED
I'm on my way.
The same song playing in one ear.
On repeat.
As loud as a jet engine.
I'll be deaf by the time I'm eighteen—
everything's perfect.

DOM
I look at the pictures on his profile—he seems all right.

FRED
It's as if the cliff is tugging me along by the collar.
And I'm there.
I check out the view—wow!

Pause. They look at the view.

Hey, looks like someone's spray-painting words on a warehouse.

DOM
They say you can do whatever you want in The City and no one cares.

FRED
Really?

DOM
That's what I heard.

    Pause.

FRED
Dom for Dominic?

DOM
Fred for Frederic?

FRED
Everyone's a comic.

DOM
My first impression of Fred—
His hair hides half his face
and he looks like he's caught in his clothes.

FRED

My first impression of Dom—
He has a shaved head, arms crossed, looking like a killer.
How's it going?

DOM

Best day of my life. You?

FRED

School starts tomorrow. I've had a stomach ache all day.
We're trying it out . . .
Here.
This is our fifth house since I learned how to count.
The cat's freaked out, it's hiding under the front steps.
It used to hunt birds and bring us all sorts of crap.
Did cat stuff, you know.
Seems like everything's my fault somehow.

DOM

Where you from?

FRED

Some hole called Way-Too-Far-From-The-City.

DOM

No wonder you moved.

FRED

It's—a bit more complicated than that.

DOM

Well. You wanted to see the view—you saw it.

FRED
We look at each other, not sure what to do.

It's awkward. A beat.

I like your hat.

DOM
It's a hat.

FRED
What are you up to now?

DOM
I'm hungry, I'm cold, and I need to take a piss.

FRED
Okay.

DOM
That's about it.

FRED
So piss. There's trees everywhere here.

Pause.

DOM
Uh. I can wait until I get home.

FRED
So that's how it starts . . .

DOM
You'll see, we've got everything in Not-The-City—
the movie theatre, the mall, the Dollarama, et cetera.

FRED
Yeah. I noticed.

DOM
He stares at me, eyes full of questions.

FRED
You shave your head?

DOM
Did it this summer.
Now the wind can't mess it up.

FRED
And I tell myself—I think I just made a new friend!

DOM
Oh, and don't go thinking we're friends now.

> DOM *and* FRED *sit there, side by side, on a concrete slab, on the*
> *edge of the cliff or on the ground.*
> *Stars appear in the sky.*

FRED
So we stay there, looking up at the stars . . .
The City's on the other side of the bridge.
The stars wink at me from above.
You never know, I might just like it here.

DOM
Well, you'd be the first.

2. This Guy from Class

FRED
The next day.

DOM
It's four o'clock, I'm at The Letters.
To do:

- Thank my razor, once again.
- Look in the fridge, eat something nasty because my whackjob mother forgot to get groceries—again.
- Call Dad, accuse him of abandoning me when I was four, just something I love doing.

But instead I look out at The City all day long.
The birds are here, just like yesterday.
Looking for french fries 'cause there's no more fish in the river.
All of a sudden, I'm thinking about . . . Fred.

FRED
Hey. How's it going?

DOM
Uh. Hi.

FRED
You up at The Letters?

DOM
Why?

FRED
Can I come?

DOM
What for?

FRED
To kill some time. With you.

DOM
It's public property.

FRED
Okay!
Tires, dog shit, rubbers . . .
And I'm there.

Pause.

I didn't see you in class today.

DOM
I'm not going back, not this year.
All that place is good for is wasting your life

and waiting for the world to end.
I'm done with that chicken coop.
I can educate myself.

FRED
Sure.
Okay.

    Pause.

Don't you want to know
what my first day was like?

DOM
"What was your first day like?"

FRED
Good!

DOM
Really.

FRED
A few guys gave me attitude—
Nothing I couldn't handle.
It took me two hours to find my locker.
Happy Hills is so huge.
And when I finally found my locker, I found Jimmy.
This guy from class.
He was there, just hanging out.

DOM
Jimmy, huh.

FRED
He showed me around—the cafeteria, et cetera.
Jimmy talks loud and fast. Puts his arm around my shoulders while
we walk.
During biology class, we rolled our eyes at exactly the same time,
twice—
I think I might've made a new friend.

DOM
I bet he introduced you to his stupid sheep, didn't he?

FRED
Edward, Jared, Andrew . . .

DOM
Jimmy was my friend, too.

FRED
What happened?

DOM
It's—private.

FRED
It was the best first day I ever had!
I uploaded a photo of me smiling.
Almost everyone in class liked it.

DOM

I'm happy for you,
I say, staring at the smog hanging over The City.

Pause.

FRED

I brought some fries.
With ketchup.
They're probably cold.
My father says it's dangerous.

DOM

Cold fries or ketchup?

FRED

The City.

DOM

Your father probably says a lot of things that aren't true.

DOM and FRED eat fries. Cold. With ketchup.

FRED

You got anything—to smoke?

DOM

Who do you think I am? Course I do.

FRED

Dom pulls out his stash and rolls in a flash—a real expert.

DOM
Puff puff puff.
Here.

FRED
Puff, puff, puff.
Cough, cough.

Pause.

Dom! Look at The City!
It looks like, like . . .
all the guys and girls have their shirts off, and are singing throat
songs . . .
There's a parade of people wearing feathers and sparkles . . .
There's tribal music, fireworks, and everyone's making out!

DOM
Yeah. They do that all the time over there.

FRED
And I start laughing.

FRED laughs.

Laughing and laughing and laughing!

DOM
What's so funny?

FRED
I don't know!

FRED *laughs even harder.*

DOM
Careful, you're gonna choke.

FRED
I double over, my stomach aches.
Dom can't help it and starts laughing, too.

> *They laugh.*
> *Share a moment.*
> *Pause.*

DOM
It must be—amazing.
To live over there.

FRED
I don't know.

DOM
Yeah you do.

FRED
Oh. Okay.

> *Pause.*

DOM
Here, in Not-The-City, people think they're living.
But they're not.
They're just living someone else's life.

The wind starts to gust. It gets cold.
Suddenly, a spotlight lights up The City on the other side of the river.
It's beautiful.

FRED

The City's so beautiful tonight!
We should go across.

DOM

The bridge won't let us.
Try it, you'll see.
We're prisoners here.

FRED

What are you talking about?
You and I are going to go across.
I know we can.

    Pause.

DOM

You want to go across—with me?

FRED

Sure. Why not?

DOM

Swear, or it's only words.

FRED

Okay.
I swear we're going to go across.
On my life.

DOM

I swear we're going to go across.
On my life.

FRED

But it has to be in June.
I need to finish the school year.

DOM

Oh, come on!

FRED

And that was that. No way Dom and I could go back now.

The wind blows and a plastic bag flies away.
It's mild out but there's still a chill in the air.
In the distance we hear a fog horn.
And the birds' piercing squawks.

3. Bitches

DOM's at The Letters. FRED's under a street light.

DOM
About two weeks go by.
At home, the phone doesn't stop ringing.
It's the old bird from school, I know it.

FRED
I always feel a bit drunk when I'm with my new friends, even
when I don't drink.

DOM
Hey, Fred for Frederic?

FRED
Like I'm floating when I walk—I'm not alone anymore.
This has been the best two weeks of my school life.

DOM
Fred?

FRED
I look at the stars.
It's going to be all right, Mom, it's going to be all right.
You can sleep up there, in your pretty yellow dress.
It won't start again, everything that happened
in Way-Too-Far-From-The-City—I'm safe.

DOM
Yoo-hoo, Alfred?

FRED
Messages from Dom are piling up—

DOM
Why aren't you answering?
Are you in the parking lot?

FRED
What do you care?

DOM
What's with you?

FRED
What? I have friends.

DOM
Who? Them?

FRED
Yeah!

DOM
Oh, is that why you're being such a jerk?

FRED
I'm not being a jerk, I'm just . . . busy.

DOM

What do you guys do out there?

FRED

We tell each other stories,
chuck peanuts and nickels at all the weirdos.
Stuff you wouldn't like.
Jimmy's looking out for me.
We check out all the fancy cars going to the mall.
One day, he's going to drive a convertible,
a red one with white trim,
and speed down the highway doing 180,
all the way to Swamp Bottom or maybe Saint Nowhere,
and then he'll take off, right at the end of the road . . .

DOM

Surrounded by *bitches*.

FRED

Hey!

DOM

It's always coming out of his mouth,
splattering on the walls—*bitches, bitches, bitches.*

FRED

(to audience) Sorry about that.

DOM

That's how Jimmy is—he doesn't know how to say "girls."
You like talking about *bitches* with your buddy Jimmy?

FRED
What are you doing?

DOM
I think I might have been wrong about you.

FRED
Meaning?

DOM
You choose—you're either my friend or Jimmy's.

FRED
I choose Jimmy.

DOM
Like I needed you anyway.
Bye, Fred for Frederic.

FRED
Yeah. Bye!

> *Pause.*

And Dom's gone.
My fingers freeze on my phone.

DOM & FRED
What did I just do?

FRED
I update my status—
"Today was a rough one. Think I just lost a friend . . . "
And everyone in my class likes it.

4. The Mirror

DOM is alone in his room. In front of a mirror.

DOM
October seventh. Night.
I'm in my room.
The House of Misery in Torture Town.
I'm in there—trying to find myself *beautiful.*
The mirror hurls insults back at me.
Hello? Where are you?
Where are you? Where's the person I'm supposed to be, *exactly*?
That person's going to show up sooner or later, right?
Making friends with Fred was the worst idea ever.
He's trying to be like everyone else, looking down on everyone.
I saw them, him and Jimmy, talking the other day.
Looking over at me.
Fred pretended to laugh, sucking up to him.
Yeah, he must be so happy with the cool kids.
Hope you're loving it, Fred, you lucky piece of shit!

Pause.

As usual, my mother's asleep in front of the TV.
I rummage through her medicine cabinet.
And I have a chemical night, finally finding some peace.

FRED's *alone in his room. Looking in the mirror.*

FRED
October seventh. Night.
I'm in my room.
My father says I go out too much. He wants to *talk*. Again.
He never understands anything and my time is precious.
I'm in there—trying to find myself *beautiful*.
My friends are in the parking lot.
They're not answering my texts.
Normally, Jimmy doesn't leave me alone,
calls me his puppy, newbie.
I'm climbing the walls.
They showed up at Dom's house and made him go back to school.
His mother didn't even know.
Everyone looks at him.
Whispering.
And I don't know what to do.
Jimmy finally spilled—
"So, you hang out with *Dom*, right?"
Yeah . . . no . . . not anymore . . .
"If I were you, I'd watch out . . . it might be contagious."
Uh. What?
"Don't you know?"
I start to shake when Jimmy tells me.
All of a sudden, my feet are stuck in cement.
And I don't sleep all night.

5. Disguises

FRED
Halloween night.

> *DOM's alone, sitting on the concrete block that also serves as a platform.*
> *He's wearing a pop diva outfit—a short little skirt, a spaghetti-strap tank top, a blond wig, a sequined jacket, a headset, and way too much makeup.*
> *Tying it all together is a proudly worn pencil-drawn moustache.*

DOM
That morning I decide to dress up like a pop star
—short skirt, crop top.
And a moustache
that says screw you to all the pop stars in the world.
And to all the giggling girls at my school
who think they're so funny and cute in their demeaning costumes.
Obviously, they made me pay for it . . .

> *FRED enters, uncomfortable, in a soldier costume: camouflage pants and jacket, boots, bullet belt, black stripes under his eyes, and topped off with a fake beard. You get the picture.*

FRED
That morning I decide to dress up like—well, like *this*.
My father helps me put it all together—and is he ever happy.
I don't know what I was thinking. Really.

Pause.

Nice skirt.

DOM
Nice beard.
Why aren't you with your "friends"?

FRED
What "friends."

DOM
Tell me.

FRED
So, after school, I meet them in the parking lot.
And all of a sudden, my stomach drops—everyone's wearing *jeans*,
and I'm the only one with a *costume*.
Help. Me. Now.
They all start snickering.
They're there, listening to music, standing around under the lights,
et cetera.
And I try to get in on the conversation.
But something's off.
I get the feeling they're talking about me behind my back.
Then, all of a sudden, Jimmy asks me, super loud—
"Hey, newbie, why aren't you wearing your *leotard*?
That'd be a perfect costume for you."
Fucking fuck. That asshole.
I showed him those pictures because I trusted him.
So, now I have to confess, in front of everyone—
I did *gymnastics* for ten years, competitions, an Olympic hopeful.

In a skin-tight bodysuit, of course.
"Hey, show us something, newbie!"
Okay . . .
And I walk on my hands.
They film me with their phones.
I do a backflip, a somersault, my routine's over, and the video's
online.
"She's so graceful!" says one of them.
Jimmy punches me in the shoulder.
Stop it!
"What? It's just a little love tap!"
That's when I hear it, between laughs . . . *the word.*

DOM
What word?

FRED
I look at Jimmy—and I understand.
I run away before I start crying.
"Get back here!" they say, laughing.
Now I'm the one they're throwing peanuts and nickels at.
The asphalt allows the word to come up and trip me.
Phones fly high and they film me.
To save face, I update my status—
"Great night with my friends!"
But the entire class knows better and leaves comments.
It's really, really over.
Long live my clique.
After everything I did to make sure it never happened again,
the same thing that happened at my last three schools . . .
I even gave up gymnastics *because of it.*

I want to kill my profile.
The one online and the other one—the real one.

Pause.

I feel like such an idiot.

DOM
You should take that off.
It doesn't suit you.

FRED
I don't have anything else to wear.

Pause.

DOM
I could lend you my skirt, if you want.

Pause.

FRED
No. Thanks.

DOM
It's Halloween.

FRED
I know. I'm not feeling it.

*Pause. A bird flies by and watches them, for a moment.
It's not buying it. It flies off.*

You still mad at me?

DOM
Yes.

FRED
Dom . . .
Jimmy told me everything.
About you.

Pause.

DOM
Probably didn't tell you much.

FRED
Go on, then. You tell me.

Pause.

DOM
What? This summer I updated my status
and asked everyone to call me he.
I've been deleting their comments one after the other ever since.
Any questions?

FRED
Ever since Jimmy told me about Dom,
I have thousands of questions wanting to burst out of me—
Are you taking hormones?
Are you going to get an operation?

DOM
Guys are idiots. I never want to be a guy.

FRED
Then what are you?

DOM
Depends on the day.
A cactus, a bird.
I want to change whenever I want,
be one or the other at the same time,
or be neither whenever I feel like it,
and dress any way I want.

Pause.

FRED
So you're like—between the two?
That's not possible.

DOM
People used to think the world was flat.

FRED
Yeah. And?

DOM
Well, that's it.

Pause.

FRED

How long have you been like this?

DOM

Ever since I can remember I've felt like—I'm not a girl.

Dresses are so uncomfortable—you can't run, you can't roll around in the mud.

I always liked playing with boys more—I was the best at baseball, the best at hockey.

When I was ten, one day, when she didn't happen to be drunk, my mother forced me to try on a bra—

"You have to be more feminine."

Really.

The shame I felt in the dressing room that day.

When I'm in girl's clothes, I'm wearing a disguise, you understand? I screamed at her—

I'm never going to be a girl!

And she knew there was no way I was going to wear that thing under my overalls.

Pause.

It doesn't matter what I am. I won't ever be like everyone else.

Not like I chose it.

This is how I am.

That's all.

The path I'm on is steep, dirty, and desperate, full of twists and turns, and totally muddy.

But it's the only one I can take.

Pause.

We're all going to end up looking the same anyway.
Like my grandparents—
They've been married fifty years and no one can tell who's who.

Pause.

FRED
It'd be weird now for me to talk about you like you're a "she."

DOM
Just keep doing what you've been doing.

Pause.

FRED
I kinda had my suspicions, you know.

DOM
Really?

FRED
You can kind of tell.

DOM
Tell what?

FRED
Uh. I don't know.

An awkward pause.
The spotlight from the other side blinds them for a moment.

Dom, what's the point of all this if you're just going to be all alone all the time?

DOM
You really don't get it, Alfred.

Pause.

FRED
Anyway . . .
I think it's cool.

DOM
Really?

FRED
Yes.

Pause. FRED sits next to DOM.

It's going to be tough avoiding my old friends all day now.

DOM
I have a part for you, Fred for Frederic.
In my R-rated horror film. I'm playing the bad guy.
I'm going to call it *Horror Hills*.
The story's kind of basic but the ending's totally amazing.
Picture this—
Heads. Everyone from school, their heads all roll around like dodge balls. Until there's this little mountain of heads, blood spurting, eyes rolling, and the whole time the little chickens keep bumping into each other, slipping and sliding in puddles of blood.

And you and I laugh, from up above, swords in our hands, watching them die in agony!

FRED
It's gonna be tough to get them to be extras!

> *They laugh.*
> *Pause.*

DOM
All right. I gotta go check if my mother's still breathing. See you, Alfred.

FRED
See you.
Dom.

> DOM *leaves.*
> FRED *watches him go.*
> *Then he leaves as well.*
> *The following conversation is displayed on the big Letters.*
> *Birds come to rest there.*

DOM
Did you look at the stars tonight?
Beautiful, huh.

FRED
Yeah.
There's one that keeps twinkling.
That must be my mother.

Pause.

DOM
What happened, to your mother?

FRED
One morning, she woke me up and told me she had something in her brain.
Something they couldn't take out.

DOM
Okay.

FRED
A month later she was gone.
By the end, she couldn't recognize me.
That's it.
After that, my father kept saying—
"Your mom needs to be here.
Nothing's possible without your mom.
Your mom needs to be here."

Pause.

Everyone hates their mother.
But there's nothing I wouldn't give to have her here.
With us.
Like before.

Pause.

6. The Person

An autumn chill has set in beneath The Letters.
DOM and FRED are there, sitting next to each other,
each with their phones, playing one of those silly games
everyone wastes so much time on.

DOM
November.

FRED
Days of the dead.

DOM
To do:

- Buy rubber boots, red ones.
- Avoid slashing my wrists.
- Find a way, IRL, to talk to *Michelle.*

So?

FRED
What?

DOM
Where were you last night?

FRED
My room.

DOM
Why didn't you come out?

FRED
Didn't feel like it.

> *A boat goes by, birds squawk.*
> DOM *stares at* FRED *intently.*

What, what's the matter?

DOM
And I see it, something's out of place, on his face—
Are you wearing eyeliner?

FRED
Who? Me?

DOM
No, your cousin, dummy!

FRED
What? No.

DOM
Yeah!

FRED
Nuh-uh.

DOM
Fred.

FRED
Okay, so it happens, once in a while.
In my room.
No big deal.
Lots of guys wear makeup—singers, et cetera.

DOM
It's not a crime.

FRED
It doesn't mean anything.

DOM
I know.

FRED
It doesn't mean anything, okay!

> *The birds fly away, scared.*
> *Pause.*

DOM
I could show you how, sometime.
I might not be a girl, but I know how to do makeup.
Don't be like that.
Maybe you're just—*a different kind of guy.*

FRED
Don't say that, Dom. Don't ever say that again.

DOM
Okay . . .

A long pause.

FRED
I looked at some pictures of The City, you'll see,
it's going to be perfect.
You can rent your own apartment there, even when you're fifteen.
We'll help each other: I'll work in a restaurant
and you'll work in a movie theatre, or the other way around.
After nine o'clock, protesters take over the streets.
Artists live in lofts and make their own clothing.
We'll buy overalls for you, skinny jeans for me.
We'll dance around burning trash cans all night long.
No one'll tell us what to do.
For once, we're gonna be really happy.

DOM
Yeah . . .

FRED
You don't think so?

DOM
Sure . . .

FRED
What's the matter?

DOM
Fred . . .

FRED
I don't like the sound of this.
What?

DOM
I have to tell you.
There's someone.
At school.
Someone who fills my belly with Jell-O and
makes me forget my name
when I walk by
them in the hallway.

FRED
Someone?

DOM
Who makes everything softer and wetter
and more meaningful.

FRED
Like?

DOM
Like, like I'm floating on a giant heart-shaped cotton cloud
or I'm on an imaginary swing that never ever stops,
and now I understand something huge and true,

but I can't talk about it with words.
It's turning my guts inside out,
it's tearing me apart.
But it doesn't hurt, no . . .
Except when it stops.
I never thought this could happen to me.
To me!

Pause.

FRED
So you're saying you're in love.

DOM
We haven't really talked yet.
But I think so.

FRED
Dom, I have a question—

DOM
It's a girl, Fred. A girl.

FRED
A girl—like a normal girl?

DOM
With arms, knees, ears, and everything.

FRED
I mean—

DOM
It's Michelle.

FRED
Michelle!

DOM
What?

FRED
I didn't know that . . .

DOM
That what?

FRED
Nothing.
That she—
That you–
That you were into—girls.

DOM
Not just.

FRED
No?

DOM
For me, it's not what's down below that matters.
It's what's above the neck, the person.
How her eyes smile,
how her lips squeeze together and she gets this cute little dimple—

FRED
Okay, I get it.

DOM
When I see her, it feels like my arms turn into these two
bulldozers.
It's strong enough to demolish bungalows, blow up Happy Hills,
make the fake rocket take off, make the prime minister's hair stand
straight up, get my mother a job, even put an end to war!

FRED
I've never seen you like this—it's serious.

DOM
What about you?

FRED
What about me?

DOM
Fred.

FRED
I don't believe in all that,
Cotton clouds, swings, et cetera.

DOM
Everybody does.

FRED

My parents stopped fighting the day
we found out my mother was going to die.
Love always ends badly.

DOM

It doesn't have to.

FRED

I just think—it's not for me.

DOM

Of course it is, dummy!
It's the one thing that actually matters!
Knowing someone somewhere loves you?
It's probably the only thing that can save us.

FRED

You're so full of it.

DOM

I need to get up the nerve to talk to her after class.

FRED

I could tell her you love her, if you want.

DOM

No you won't!

FRED
What? If it'll help . . .

DOM
You're the only person I've told.
Don't say a word to anyone, okay.

FRED
Why Michelle?

DOM
I mean, she's pretty.

FRED
Well, duh.

DOM
And she's the only one who wrote me since I started using "he"
and said she thought it was cool.

FRED
I said I thought it was cool!

DOM
It's not the same with you.

Somewhere a pile of dead leaves falls.

FRED
What'll you two do?

DOM
What do you mean?

FRED
You and her?

DOM
Like everyone—the movie theatre, the mall, the Dollarama—

FRED
Et cetera.

DOM
That's right.

> *Pause.*

FRED
I'm happy for you, Dom.
Sounds like—you found the one.

> *The wind picks up. Shivers.*

7. Lobotomy

DOM and FRED are both somewhere other than The Letters.

FRED

And then, at the end of the term, I read—
"Dom is now in a relationship with Michelle."

DOM

After that, Fred got weird.
And I got happy!
Where are you, Alfred the magnificent?
I need to talk to someone about how happy I am.
I'm happy, I'm happy, I'm superfabulafantastamazingly happy!
I'm so happy I'm even making up words!
Why don't we go to The Letters anymore?

FRED

I answer—
"It's cold out.
Had a big argument with my dad yesterday.
Need to get good marks on my exams."

DOM

Or what? You gonna turn into a unicorn?

FRED

A unicorn—LOL.

DOM
They're asking us to decide what we want to be.
Seriously. We're only fourteen.
Like we should already be signing our death sentences.
My dream is to be as useless as possible to society.

FRED
Doesn't it bother your mother that you spend half the school day
at the mall with—*your girlfriend?*

DOM
My mother's on antidepressants. I don't think she can even read
anymore.
Come out.

FRED
Well, it's important to succeed in life.

DOM
Succeed at what?
Buying a townhouse before you're twenty five?

FRED
That's what you're going to end up doing with—*your girlfriend.*

DOM
You should be happy for us!

FRED
Ugh. He's using *us*!
Kill. Me. Now.

DOM
We, Michelle and I . . . we saw these skinny jeans that would look really good on you, we did, Fred.

FRED
You *two* shouldn't bother—
That's all over with anyway.

DOM
What do you mean?

FRED
I just want to be normal now.
Normal, you understand?

DOM
So you're giving up?

FRED
I never wanted to fight in the first place.

DOM
Did they give you a lobotomy?

FRED
Bye.

DOM
Okay, bye!

They both throw their phones. Violently.

8. Love

DOM is at The Letters.

DOM
To do in the new year:

- Burn the present my father sent me.
- Go across to The City . . .
- Keep heading as far south as possible until we see monkeys and parrots and it's hot all year long.
- Walk bare-chested because it's really not fair that we can't.
- Get married.
- Live happily ever after and have lots of kids.

FRED
So. Anyway.

DOM
We both ended up at The Letters, on January fifteenth.

FRED
Didn't plan on it.

DOM
Minus a thousand up on the cliff.

FRED
What are you doing here?

DOM
Normally people say, "Hey, how are you?"

FRED
"Hey, how are you?"

DOM
I hate them.
You?

FRED
Me too.
Okay. So who and why?

DOM
You're not the only one who's got a word, Fred for Frederic.
Ours has four letters and it rhymes with "bike."
I was having lunch with Michelle the other day—a love sandwich with a side of joy yogurt.
And then Jared came over and said it, just like that—I got up and squeezed his balls so hard he started to cry.
Obviously, the old bird made me stay in her office.
"Think about what you've done, *young lady.*"
Something's rotting in there. Like an old black banana someone tossed inside a year ago. You have to close the door fast as possible to keep the stink in. It's a torture device to make criminals confess.
Old forgotten bananas are disgusting.
Even I wouldn't eat one.
A few hours later, she came back and threatened me with her huge feathers.

"Are you ready to apologize, *young lady*?"
Never!
What a bunch of chickens!

> *Pause.*
> *A winter wind stirs the branches.*
> *The City, on the other side, is very, very quiet.*

I'm happy to see you, Fred.

FRED
Sure, whatever.

DOM
Your eyes seem different.

FRED
They're hiding from the cold.

DOM
It can be hot out if you want it to be.

FRED
How?

DOM
All you have to do is believe.
And then it happens.

FRED
You're so full of it.

Pause.

DOM
Okay, Fred for Frederic.
What's going on?

FRED
I'm cold, Jimmy is on my case again,
and ever since my best friend got a girlfriend,
I'm alone all the time.
Any questions?

DOM
You should fall in love too, Fred—it would help.

FRED
Looking at you, I'm not so sure.

DOM
It's wonderful, the other night at the movies—

FRED
Jimmy won't stop bugging me—

DOM
Michelle held onto me during this chase scene—

FRED

He always tries to smack my ass when I walk by—

DOM

I held her hand just before it was over—

FRED

I'm dreaming about chainsaws—

DOM

We tried counting the stars in the parking lot—

FRED

I'm like my mother was before she died—

DOM

We kissed beneath the street light—

FRED

I have something in my brain that can't be taken out.

Pause.

DOM

Fred . . .

I think—I want to go across to The City with Michelle.

9. The Actor

FRED takes a step forward, alone, facing the emptiness, hair flying in the wind, at the entrance to the bridge.

FRED
Here I am, all alone, about to cross the bridge.
Worst night of my life since taking my first steps.
I started believing in hell since going to that school.
Even my mirror spits in my face.
Dom's with his girlfriend.
Of course—*you can't be alone on Valentine's Day.*
My soul aches.
I have to get the fuck out of here.
The City's calling from the other side—*come here, come here.*
I'm freezing in this little jacket.
I'm such an idiot!
A stupid, dumb fa—

Pause.

It's up there watching me.
What are you looking at, Bridge?
I'll cross you if I want to, okay!
So why haven't I?
You just watch me.
I take a step forward.
The City lights twinkle, far away.
They don't need big letters to let people know they exist.
They don't give a crap about us in The City.

Like Dom doesn't give a crap about me—
I hope you're happy and all romantic with *your girlfriend*!
With every step I take, the bridge just gets longer and longer.
It's endless.

We hear a low rumbling, like a big dog growling.

All of a sudden everything starts to shake beneath my feet.
And there's this growling, like, like—a big dog!

A storm rages: snow pelts him in the face.
Spotlights blind him.

You don't scare me, Bridge!
I move forward.
I move forward.
I don't go back.
But with every step, The City is a little farther away.

The growling gets louder, the snowstorm more violent.

I'm swallowing snow by the shovelful.
Every day . . . there's this actor who takes over my body. He's
here—he's always here—he's a guy *who's playing a guy* who tries to
be bigger, stronger, more *manly*, who likes what all the other *guys
like*, speaks with a deep voice, makes sure he never *lets his guard
down*, a guy who's always stiff like he just swallowed an ironing
board, wears clothes that are too baggy even if it's ugly, and does
everything to make sure no one notices *something isn't quite right*
with him.

It isn't that complicated—I just want to be a guy, do you understand, Bridge? Just—*a guy*, like a guy. I just want to be a guy, just a—guy— Ahh!

He screams.
It's as if the entire world is quaking and poor FRED *struggles against it like he's fighting for his life.*

The railing isn't that high.
The river flowing beneath my feet is icy and black . . .
I'll jump off.
Yes.
Then it'll all be over.
Not like anyone would miss me.
Just leave without a trace.
I'll meet you up there, Mom.

We no longer see anything.
Long pause.
He might have actually done it.

Yeah, well . . .
Fine. I'm turning around. You happy now, Bridge?

Everything goes back to normal.

The entire time, Not-The-City
was a few steps away, right behind me.
And I was back before I knew it.

Pause.

10. Clothes

FRED
Beginning of March.

DOM
Come on. Let's go out.

FRED
Who? Me?

DOM
No, your cousin, dummy!

FRED
Where to?

DOM
The mall.

FRED
Since when are you talking to me?

DOM
I want to buy a new hat.
And maybe we'll find you—a tank top.

FRED
Why don't you go with *your girlfriend*?

DOM
She's been acting weird lately.

FRED
So you're only going to be my friend when your girlfriend's acting weird?

DOM
Maybe.

FRED
Screw you!

DOM
What? I've got problems.

FRED
You're the most selfish guy I know!

DOM
I'm not a guy.

FRED
Dom drags me along.
To the mall.

Mall music.

Carbon copy salesgirls who are all gonna end up deaf thanks to the music they pump in so it feels like you're high in a dance club and not actually looking for pants.

Old people just sitting around, talking to themselves.
The same people eating the same cardboard burger with the same
soft drink that gives you zits.

DOM
You're right, it's gross here, let's go.

FRED
I thought you wanted a new hat?

DOM
I don't want a new hat, not anymore, new hats suck.

FRED
It's impossible to keep up with you.

DOM
Yeah, I know, I'm messed up. I'm really, really messed up, Fred, you
happy now?
I can't breathe. Come on. Let's go.

FRED
Dom steals a package of jujubes from the candy store.

DOM
Supplies, for tonight.
Hurry up, Alfred.
Let's go watch the sunset
and feel sorry for ourselves on top of the cliff.

FRED
Wait for me, Dom!

Then they vanish in a storm.

11. Birds

At dawn DOM *and* FRED *are back at The Letters.*
The birds squawk quietly.
It's freezing.

FRED
A few days later, I read—
"Dom is no longer in a 'relationship' and is 'single.'"

Pause.

What happened?

DOM
You wouldn't understand.

FRED
Try me.

DOM
We talked all night last night.
I could've cried out every tear in my body and died.
She says she's really happy when she's with me.

That I was kind, that I was funny, that I was attentive.
She says she loves me,
she loves me, Fred!
She says I make her laugh with my cotton clouds
and my bulldozer arms.
I told her about that, told her how I was a bigger person
when I was with her.
But even with everything—
the butterflies in our bellies,
the messages we send every eight seconds,
my name in lipstick on her bedroom mirror,
even with all that,

. . .
She can't.

FRED
What?

DOM
Be . . .
with "a girl who's pretending to be a guy."
And with all the comments and looks from other people.
At our legs walking and our hands holding.
At her profile page.
And in real life.
When I was with her I actually felt like showing up to school
every morning.
You were right—love always ends badly.

Pause.

FRED
Things aren't exactly peachy for me either,
if it makes you feel any better.

DOM
It doesn't.

FRED
I almost killed myself.

DOM
What?

FRED
The night of Valentine's Day.
I almost jumped.
Off the bridge.

DOM
What?

FRED
But I changed my mind.
Death is a bit too . . . permanent.

DOM
Don't do that ever again.

FRED
Okay.
I'm— I'm sorry.

DOM
It's okay.

Pause.

FRED
When I was on the bridge, I told myself:
If I survive the fall,
maybe I'll be *normal* after, because of the shock.
Maybe that's all I need.

A long pause.

DOM
I know what you need.

FRED
I don't feel like smoking now.

DOM
That's not what I'm talking about.

FRED
Then what?

DOM
Fred.

FRED
No.

Pause.

Stop.
Don't be stupid.
Never gonna happen.

DOM
Come on. Let's do it.

FRED
No.

DOM
We'll show them!

FRED
Today? In front of everyone?

DOM
You've been talking about it long enough!

Pause. A sigh. Something gives.

FRED
Okay . . .

DOM
Yes.

FRED
I'm scared!

DOM
I know.

FRED

What are they going to think? What are they going to say?
What are they going to—

DOM

They're just a bunch of stupid chickens!
Just picture everyone naked.

FRED

Good idea!

> DOM *takes out some eyeliner.*

DOM

Face me.

FRED

I don't know.

DOM

We can wait until tomorrow, if you want.

FRED

No! Today's the day.

DOM

Look up.
And don't move.

> DOM *does his best to draw a line under* FRED's *eyes, cheered on by*
> *The Letters and the cliff.*

FRED
How . . . how does it look?

DOM
Hey, Fred!

FRED
Dom has his phone out in a flash.

DOM
And I take a selfie, to capture the moment.

FRED
There's someone in the picture
who looks like me.
But better.
That guy is who I am.
I am that guy.

DOM
All of a sudden, the birds gather above us, wings flapping, applauding us.

Pause.

FRED
And I do it.
My father drives us to school and I tell him, "You don't need to worry, Dad."
Then I walk into class, like this.
. . .
And then . . .

Pause.

DOM
Nothing.

FRED
Well, sure, Jimmy and his sheep make their usual comments.

DOM
No worse than before.

FRED
At lunchtime, people I don't even know come up to me and ask if I want to listen to music after school.

DOM
You're—really beautiful.

FRED
Who, me?

DOM
No, your cousin, dummy!

FRED
You think so?

DOM
I've never seen you look this beautiful.

FRED
I'm embarrassed.

DOM
Me too.

Pause.

FRED
You too.

DOM
Me too?

FRED
Yes. You too.

Pause . . . It's pretty awkward.

Did we just make the spring come, Dom?

DOM
Are you nuts? It's still freezing.

FRED
Like you said, it can be hot out if you want it to.
Look, Dom!
Look, the sun's coming out.
The temperature's going up, up to thirty, thirty-five degrees.
Snow's melting all around us.
Melting as we watch.
Giant palm trees are sprouting in the streets and knocking over houses.
The schoolyard's covered in sand.
The river's turned into an ocean, Dom.

See for yourself, if you don't believe me.
No one's ever seen waves like this before.
People are coming and putting up umbrellas.
They're selling cotton candy and beer.
Actually, they're giving it away for free, even to minors!
Your mother (See? She's not so bad.) and my father are catching
some rays, and for once they're smiling at us.
No more winter jackets—we've got bathing suits on.
What kind are you wearing, Dom?

DOM
Just shorts. I don't have boobs, anyway.

DOM holds FRED's hand.

FRED
That's okay, I don't either.
We're both here, wearing shorts, and we run into the ocean.
The water's warm, the fish are warm, the sharks are leaving us
alone,
we're getting burnt to a crisp but who cares.
At the crest of a wave, we give everyone the finger. SCREW YOU!
No more laws, not anymore, even gravity can't keep us down now!
We don't care what anyone thinks.
We get carried far, far away, Dom.
We swim with the jellyfish. They say jellyfish are immortal.
We turn into jellyfish and become immortal, too.
It sure is hot out, isn't it, Dom?

DOM
I've never been so hot in all my life.

While FRED *was speaking, absolutely everything appeared: palm trees, jellyfish, cotton candy . . .*
They float in the ocean *with their shirts off.*
Their smiles say "screw you."

FRED
Dom?

DOM
What, Fred?

FRED
Are you holding my hand?

> DOM *quickly lets go of* FRED's *hand.*

DOM
I'm, I'm . . . sorry.

> *Pause.*

FRED
It's okay.

DOM
Don't think that—

FRED
That what?

DOM
I mean—

FRED
Of course not!

DOM
Because, you know—

FRED
I know!
There's no way we could ever actually date, Dom.

Pause.

DOM
Why not?

FRED
Well because . . .
How would it . . .
What would I *be*?

DOM
I don't know. But I'm sure we'd figure it out!

They laugh.
Pause.
They stop laughing.

Hey, I didn't tell you. The old bird called me to her office.
First time anyone ever praised me for anything at school.
And all I did was show up for class.
I said it was your fault. I had to defend you.

FRED

Very funny.

DOM

Compliments lead to buying bungalows.
We're not going to be like them, huh, Alfred?

FRED

No matter what, Dom,
we're never going to be like them.

12. The Bridge

And now DOM *and* FRED *are on the side of the bridge
that separates Not-The-City from The City.*

DOM

So here we are,
June twenty-third
to do . . .

- Walk across the bridge.

With Fred.

FRED

I've had a stomach ache all day.
What if we don't make it?

DOM
We just have to really believe, take a step.
And we'll make it.

Pause.

FRED
What are we going to do, over there?

DOM
We'll see when we get there.

First deep breath.

FRED
Guess what? Jimmy tried to kiss me.

DOM
No way!

FRED
In the locker room, after gym.
He was taking a very long time to get changed.
It was weird, he was shaking.
I didn't know what to do, so I put my hand up to stop him.
And that worked.
He turned around and left.

DOM
Way to go, Fred!

Pause.

All right, ready?

FRED
I don't know anymore.
What if we fall?

DOM
We can't fall, Fred. We're together.
Come *on*.
Let's just see if it's really better over there.
We can always come back.

FRED
Yeah. You're right. Let's do it.
We can always come back.

DOM
Yeah.

Second deep breath.

FRED
Dom . . .

DOM
Fred, no more questions—

FRED
Thanks. Dom.

Pause.

DOM
Why?

FRED
I don't know.
Just 'cause.

>   *Pause.*

DOM
No problem.

>   *Third deep breath.*

FRED
So, here we are—

DOM
Fred and me—

FRED
Holding hands until they bleed—

DOM
Houses are behind us, sulking—

FRED
The movie theatre, the mall, the Dollarama—

DOM
The big Letters—

FRED

The birds who saw all our tears—

DOM

And we both take a step—

DOM & FRED

Onto the bridge that leads to The City, on the other side of the river.

The end.

Acknowledgements

This translation was developed with the support of Playwrights' Workshop Montréal at the Glassco Translation Residency in Tadoussac.

We'd also like thank Youtheatre, in particular Michel Lefebvre, for commissioning the translation.

Author and translator Olivier Sylvestre holds a bachelor's degree in criminology from the University of Montreal and a diploma in playwriting from the National Theatre School of Canada. With Hamac he has published the récit *le désert* and *noms fictifs*, a finalist for the 2018 Governor General's Literary Award, and two plays, *La loi de la gravité* and *Guide d'éducation sexuelle pour le nouveau millénaire*. *La loi de la gravité* has been translated into German and won the ARTCENA Creation Assistance Award (France) and the Coburger Autorenforum Award (Germany). Olivier also works as a writing instructor and dramaturg. He lives in Montréal.

Bobby Theodore is a Toronto-based screenwriter, playwright, dramaturg, and translator. After graduating from the National Theatre School of Canada's playwriting section in 1998, he was a finalist for the Governor General's Literary Award in 2000 for his translation of *15 Seconds* by François Archambault. Since then, Bobby has gone on to translate over twenty-five plays from French to English. His most recent translations include *The Just* by Albert Camus and *Public Enemy* by Olivier Choinière.

First edition: April 2021
Printed and bound in Canada by Rapido Books, Montreal

Jacket art by Raz Latif
Author photo © Patrick Palmer
Translator photo © Keith Barker

PLAYWRIGHTS
CANADA PRESS

202-269 Richmond St. W.
Toronto, ON
M5V 1X1

416.703.0013
info@playwrightscanada.com
www.playwrightscanada.com
@playcanpress